W9-DID-765

Sharks

A Buddy Book by
Deborah Coldiron

ABDO
Publishing Company

UNDERWATER WORLD

VISIT US AT
www.abdopublishing.com

Published by ABDO Publishing Company, 8000 West 78th Street, Edina, Minnesota 55439.

Copyright © 2009 by Abdo Consulting Group, Inc. International copyrights reserved in all countries. No part of this book may be reproduced in any form without written permission from the publisher. Buddy Books™ is a trademark and logo of ABDO Publishing Company.

Printed in the United States.

Coordinating Series Editor: Sarah Tieck
Contributing Editor: Michael P. Goecke
Graphic Design: Deborah Coldiron
Cover Photograph: Seapics.com
Interior Photographs/Illustrations: Brandon Cole Marine Photography (pages 16, 27, 29); Corbis (pages 9, 15, 17, 22); Digital Vision (pages 9, 15, 30); Jeff Rotman Photography (pages 7, 22, 23, 24); Minden Pictures: Flip Nicklin (page 16), Norbert Wu (page 19); NOAA (page 16); Peter Arnold Inc.: Jeffrey L. Rotman (page 23); Photos.com (pages 17, 19); SeaPics.com: (pages 7, 17, 21, 24, 25, 28); SIMoN: Chad King (pages 9, 17), MBARI (page 23); Wikipedia.org - Wikipedia Commons: Chris Gotshalk (page 25), Terry Gross (page 9)

Library of Congress Cataloging-in-Publication Data

Coldiron, Deborah.
   Sharks / Deborah Coldiron.
      p. cm. -- (Underwater world)
   Includes index.
   ISBN 978-1-60453-138-1
   1. Sharks--Juvenile literature. I. Title.

QL638.9.C57 2009
597.3 -- dc22

                                                            2008005052

Table Of Contents

The World Of Sharks

   Every living creature needs water. Some animals not only need water, they live in it, too.

   Scientists have found more than 250,000 kinds of plants and animals living underwater. And, they believe there could be one million more! The shark is one animal that makes its home in this underwater world.

Water covers 70 percent of Earth's surface.

Sharks are ocean predators. They are famous for their sharp teeth and **streamlined** bodies.

The smallest sharks grow to be about 8 inches (20 cm) long. The largest can be more than 40 feet (12 m) in length!

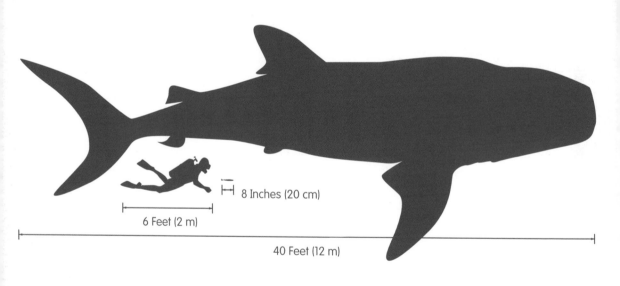

8 Inches (20 cm)

6 Feet (2 m)

40 Feet (12 m)

Whale sharks are the largest sharks. These gentle giants are not a threat to humans.

An adult spined pygmy shark is about 8 inches (20 cm) long. It is one of the world's smallest sharks.

There are around 400 shark **species** in our underwater world. Most sharks live in the salty ocean. But, a few species can enter **brackish** water or freshwater.

FAST FACTS

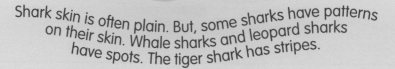

Shark skin is often plain. But, some sharks have patterns on their skin. Whale sharks and leopard sharks have spots. The tiger shark has stripes.

Tiger shark

Great white shark

Lemon shark

Blue shark

Mako shark

Whale shark

Leopard shark

Whitetip reef shark

River Sharks

A few sharks spend their entire lives in freshwater. These rare creatures are called river sharks. All river shark **species** are **endangered**.

Very little is known about these unusual sharks. Scientists believe there are at least six **unique** species. They say most can grow to be seven to ten feet (2 to 3 m) long.

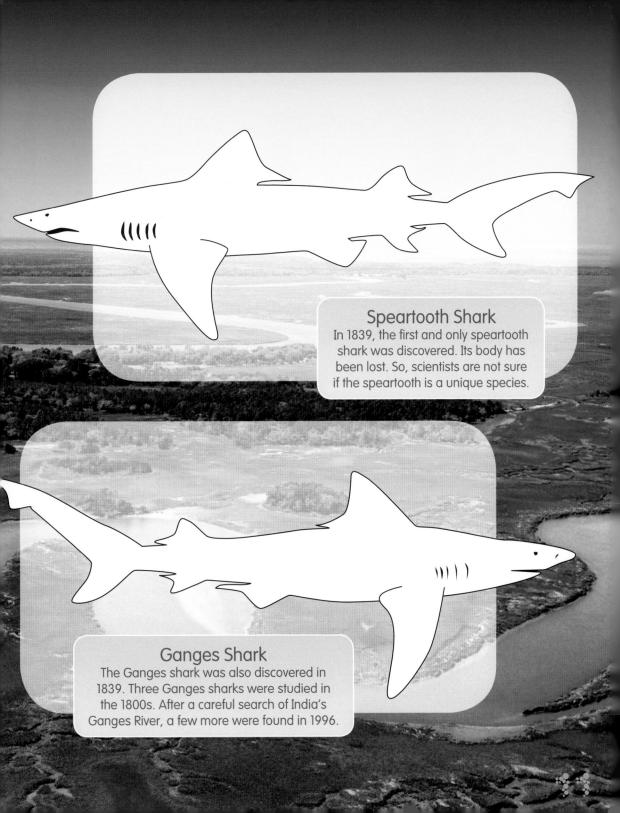

Speartooth Shark
In 1839, the first and only speartooth shark was discovered. Its body has been lost. So, scientists are not sure if the speartooth is a unique species.

Ganges Shark
The Ganges shark was also discovered in 1839. Three Ganges sharks were studied in the 1800s. After a careful search of India's Ganges River, a few more were found in 1996.

A Closer Look

A shark's skin looks smooth, but it is actually quite rough. Toothlike scales called denticles cover the shark's skin. They help protect the shark. Scientists believe denticles may also help the shark swim faster.

FAST FACTS

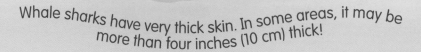

Whale sharks have very thick skin. In some areas, it may be more than four inches (10 cm) thick!

The Body Of A Shark

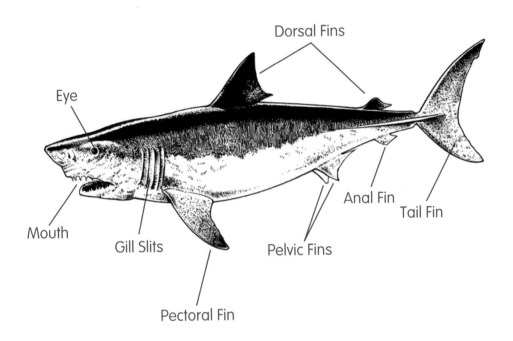

Dorsal Fins

Eye

Mouth

Gill Slits

Pectoral Fin

Pelvic Fins

Anal Fin

Tail Fin

Most sharks have a pointy or rounded **snout**. Instead of hard bone, their skeletons are made of **cartilage**. Rows of sharp teeth fill their mouths.

All sharks have a powerful tail that helps them swim. Their fins help them steer.

FAST FACTS

Like all sharks, a great white shark's jaws are not attached to its skull. When it attacks, its jaws can move in and out of its mouth. This protects the shark from injury.

Shark-O-Rama

There is great variety among shark **species**. Scientists organize the many species based on their features.

Bluntnose sixgill sharks have six gill openings.

Angel sharks' eyes are on top of their flattened bodies.

Dogfish have two dorsal fins and no anal fin.

Saw sharks have long, tooth-covered snouts.

Blue sharks have membranes that protect their eyes when they attack prey.

Nurse sharks spend a lot of time near the ocean floor. So, people sometimes call them carpet sharks.

Horned sharks have large heads and short snouts.

Great white sharks are one type of mackerel shark. They have long snouts. Their mouths reach back behind their eyes.

A Growing Shark

All newborn sharks are known as pups. But, not all pups are born the same way.

Some young sharks develop inside egg cases. Female sharks find a place to hide their eggs. Then, they leave them to hatch. Horned sharks, cat sharks, swell sharks, and Port Jackson sharks lay egg cases.

FAST FACTS Sometimes, empty egg cases wash onto shore. These are called mermaid's purses or Devil's purses.

Most shark egg cases are long and smooth *(above)*. But, the horned shark's egg cases are screw shaped *(below)*. This shape makes it easier to secure the cases between rocks.

Most often, pups develop in eggs inside their mother. There, pups receive food from the eggs or directly from the mother's body. When they are ready to be born, the female shark delivers her pups into the ocean.

Many sharks are predators even before birth. Some shark pups eat the other eggs inside their mother's body. And, gray nurse sharks may eat other newly hatched pups!

Lemon sharks give birth to live pups, just like bull sharks and Caribbean reef sharks.

Family Connections

Sharks are elasmobranchs. Elasmobranchs have five to seven **gill slits**. Their skeletons are made of **cartilage**. This group also includes skates and rays.

There are more than 500 species of rays.

Stingrays have round or diamond-shaped bodies. They also have poisonous tail spines. Blue-spotted stingrays are covered in bright blue dots.

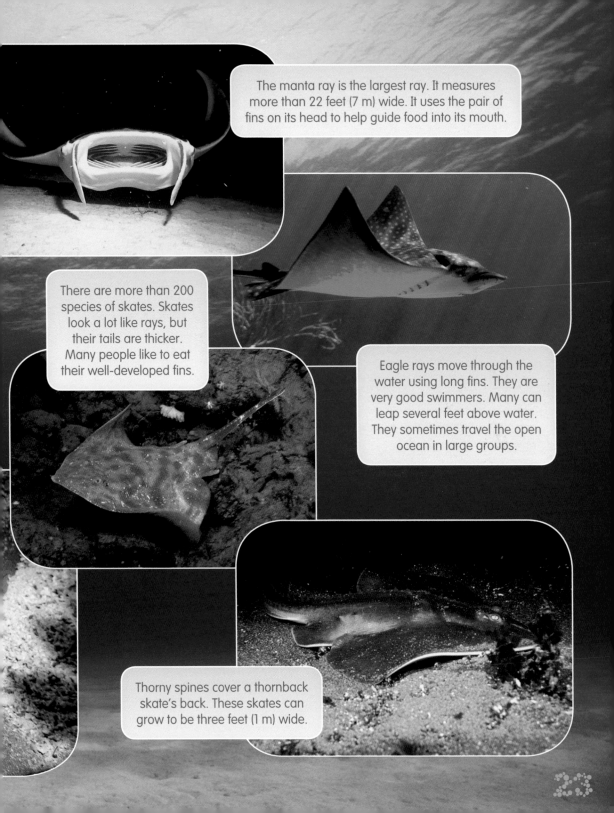

The manta ray is the largest ray. It measures more than 22 feet (7 m) wide. It uses the pair of fins on its head to help guide food into its mouth.

There are more than 200 species of skates. Skates look a lot like rays, but their tails are thicker. Many people like to eat their well-developed fins.

Eagle rays move through the water using long fins. They are very good swimmers. Many can leap several feet above water. They sometimes travel the open ocean in large groups.

Thorny spines cover a thornback skate's back. These skates can grow to be three feet (1 m) wide.

Dinnertime

Most sharks that live in the open ocean eat fast-moving creatures. Their diet includes squid, fish, and other sharks. Sharks living near the seafloor hunt bottom-dwelling clams and crabs.

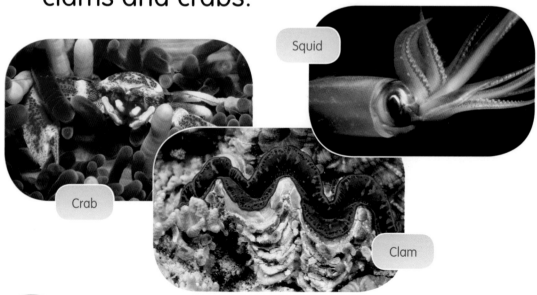

Squid

Crab

Clam

Some sharks are **filter** feeders. They swim with their mouths open wide. Much like whales, they filter **plankton** from the water to eat.

Basking sharks *(right)* and whale sharks *(below)* are the ocean's biggest fish. These filter-feeding sharks can look frightening with their large, open mouths. But, they won't harm humans.

A World Of Danger

Shark populations in the world's oceans are rapidly getting smaller. Each year, humans kill an average of 38 million sharks for food or sport. As a result, about half of all shark **species** are **endangered**.

Many sharks are killed each year for their fins. Dried shark fins are often used to make soup.

Fascinating Facts

Shark attacks are rare. Still, several **species** have bitten humans. Bull, great white, and tiger sharks are the most common attackers. Scientists believe sharks attack when they mistake people for seals or fish.

Scientists believe some sharks group with other sharks of the same size. Groups may even include different species of sharks.

Whitetip reef sharks sometimes feed in large groups at night.

➤ Sharks have changed very little in millions of years. Modern sharks resemble shark fossils dating back 100 million years!

➤ Bull sharks usually live in the ocean. But, these large sharks have been spotted in South America's Amazon River. Some have been seen in the United States's Mississippi River, too!

Great white sharks are often blamed for the occasional human attack. However, bull sharks (right) are more likely responsible.

Learn And Explore

   Can a female shark have pups without a male? In 2001, scientists at Nebraska's Henry Doorly Zoo got a shock. They discovered a hammerhead shark pup in their aquarium.

   Its mother had not been in contact with a male for more than three years. A test later showed that the pup had no father.

Most female sharks do not reproduce when they are alone. Scientists say such a case is rare.

IMPORTANT WORDS

brackish somewhat salty.

cartilage the tough, bendable matter that forms part of a skeleton.

endangered in danger of no longer existing.

filter to separate matter from air or water.

gill slit an opening that allows water to enter a fish's body and flow over its gills.

plankton small animals and plants that float in a body of water.

snout the part of an animal's head that projects forward and contains the mouth, the jaws, and the nose.

species living things that are very much alike.

streamlined having a shape that reduces the resistance to motion when moving through air or water.

unique being the only one of its kind.

WEB SITES

To learn more about sharks, visit ABDO Publishing Company on the World Wide Web. Web sites about sharks are featured on our Book Links page. These links are routinely monitored and updated to provide the most current information available.

www.abdopublishing.com

INDEX

JR. GRAPHIC FAMOUS EXPLORERS

John Cabot

Steven Roberts

PowerKiDS
press™

New York

Published in 2013 by The Rosen Publishing Group, Inc.

29 East 21st Street, New York, NY 10010

First Edition

Editor: Joanne Randolph

Book Design: Planman Technologies

Illustrations: Planman Technologies

Library of Congress Cataloging-in-Publication Data

Roberts, Steven, 1955-

John Cabot / by Steven Roberts. — 1st ed.

   p. cm. — (Jr. graphic famous explorers)

Includes index.

ISBN 978-1-4777-0072-3 (library binding) — ISBN 978-1-4777-0129-4 (pbk.) — ISBN 978-1-4777-0130-0 (6-pack)

1. Cabot, John, d. 1499—Juvenile literature. 2. America—Discovery and exploration—British—Juvenile literature. 3. North America—Discovery and exploration—British—Juvenile literature. 4. Explorers—America—Biography—Juvenile literature. 5. Explorers—Great Britain—Biography—Juvenile literature. 6. Explorers—Italy—Biography—Juvenile literature. 7. Cabot, John, d. 1499—Comic books, strips, etc. 8. America—Discovery and exploration—British—Comic books, strips, etc. 9. North America—Discovery and exploration—British—Comic books, strips, etc. 10. Explorers—America—Biography—Comic books, strips, etc. 11. Explorers—Great Britain—Biography—Comic books, strips, etc. 12. Explorers—Italy—Biography—Comic books, strips, etc. 13. Graphic novels. I. Title.

E129.C1R63 2013

970.01'5092—dc23

[B]

2012018691

Manufactured in the United States of America

CPSIA Compliance Information: Batch # W13PK1: For Further Information contact Rosen Publishing, New York, New York at 1-800-237-9932

Contents

Introduction

The late 1400s marked the dawn of European exploration. Columbus discovered the New World, and the seafaring powers of Europe were competing to find new trade routes to Asia. England had not yet emerged as a sea power and was looking for an experienced **navigator**. It would find that man in John Cabot. The story of John Cabot, however, is one of the great mysteries of exploration. None of his maps or records have survived. What little we know about him has been pieced together by letters from his friends and the work of **historians**.

Main Characters

John Cabot (c. 1450–c. 1499) An Italian navigator and explorer. He sailed to what is today Newfoundland, Canada, becoming the first European to set foot in North America since the Vikings.

Mattea Cabot (c. 1460s–c. 1500s) John Cabot's wife, with whom he had three children.

Sebastian Cabot (c. 1476–1557) John Cabot's youngest son, who also became an explorer.

John Day (c. 1460s–c. 1500s) A **merchant** from Bristol, England, and friend of John Cabot. His letters are one of the sources of information about John Cabot's voyages.

Raimondo de Soncino (c. 1460s–c. 1500s) Served as the **ambassador** from Milan, Italy, to England and a friend of John Cabot. A letter he wrote is the main source of information about Cabot's most famous voyage.

King Henry VII (1457–1509) The king of England. He financed John Cabot's voyages.

Gaspar Corte Real (c. 1450–c. 1501) A Portuguese explorer who sailed to Canada a couple of years after Cabot.

JOHN CABOT

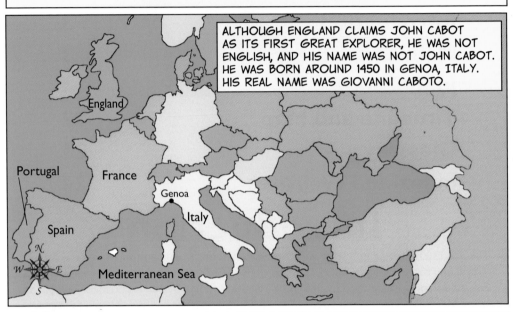

ALTHOUGH ENGLAND CLAIMS JOHN CABOT AS ITS FIRST GREAT EXPLORER, HE WAS NOT ENGLISH, AND HIS NAME WAS NOT JOHN CABOT. HE WAS BORN AROUND 1450 IN GENOA, ITALY. HIS REAL NAME WAS GIOVANNI CABOTO.

IN HIS LATE TEENS, GIOVANNI WORKED AS A MERCHANT. HE TRAVELED BY LAND TO MECCA, THE MUSLIM HOLY CITY, AND LEARNED THE TRADE ROUTES BETWEEN ASIA AND EUROPE.

SOON GIOVANNI BECAME A SAILOR. HE LEARNED THE TRADE ROUTES BETWEEN THE GREAT PORTS OF EUROPE ON THE MEDITERRANEAN SEA.

CABOT DID NOT GET FAR. WHAT LITTLE IS KNOWN OF THIS VOYAGE IS FROM A LETTER WRITTEN BY HIS FRIEND JOHN DAY TO CHRISTOPHER COLUMBUS.

YOUR LORDSHIP, HERE IS WHAT HAPPENED AS **RELATED** TO ME BY CAPTAIN CABOT.

SOON AFTER HE SET OUT TO SEA, CABOT'S SHIP RAN INTO BAD WEATHER.

HE WILL GET US ALL KILLED!

HE IS NOT EVEN ENGLISH! WE CAN'T TRUST HIM.

THE CREWMEN, WHO HAD NEVER SAILED INTO UNKNOWN WATERS BEFORE, BECAME FRIGHTENED AND TURNED AGAINST CABOT.

CABOT TURNED THE SHIP AROUND AND RETURNED TO PORT.

ALL MY WORK AND PLANNING WASTED. HOW COULD THIS HAVE HAPPENED?

KING HENRY STILL HAD CONFIDENCE IN CABOT AND DECIDED TO FINANCE A SECOND VOYAGE.

FOR KING AND COUNTRY, YOUR HIGHNESS. I WILL NOT FAIL THIS TIME.

WE MUST TRY AGAIN, JOHN.

CABOT WAS GIVEN A THREE-MASTED SHIP CALLED THE *MATTHEW*, A CREW OF 18 ABLE SEAMEN, AND ENOUGH SUPPLIES TO LAST FOR SEVERAL MONTHS.

MEN, DO YOU HAVE WHAT IT TAKES? IT WILL BE A LONG, HARD VOYAGE.

WE'RE WITH YOU, CAPTAIN!

AYE, CAPTAIN!

THE *MATTHEW* SET SAIL FROM BRISTOL, ENGLAND, ON MAY 22, 1497.

THIS TIME, CABOT WOULD NOT RISK FAILING. HE SAILED FIRST TO THE COAST OF IRELAND AND DROPPED ANCHOR. THERE HE TOOK READINGS OF HIS POSITION AND THE WEATHER, USING HIS INSTRUMENTS AND OBSERVING THE NORTH STAR.

AFTER GAINING HIS **BEARINGS**, CABOT SET OUT INTO UNKNOWN WATERS.

ON JUNE 24, 1497, CABOT STEPPED FOOT ON SHORE AND RAISED THE FLAG OF KING HENRY VII.

I HEREBY CLAIM THIS LAND IN THE NAME OF ENGLAND.

GOD BLESS THE KING AND OUR CAPTAIN!

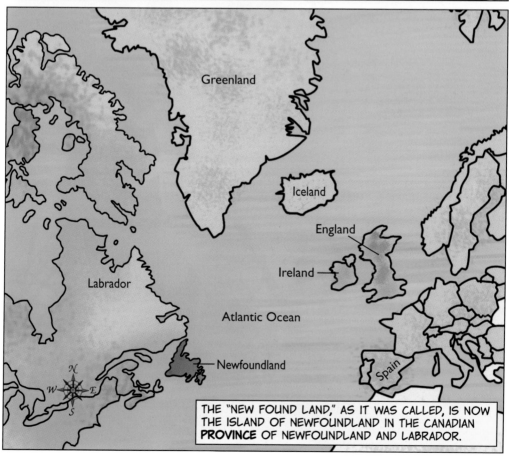

THE "NEW FOUND LAND," AS IT WAS CALLED, IS NOW THE ISLAND OF NEWFOUNDLAND IN THE CANADIAN **PROVINCE** OF NEWFOUNDLAND AND LABRADOR.

CABOT AND HIS CREW EXPLORED THE SHORE AND FOUND SIGNS OF NATIVE LIFE. THEY FOUND THE REMAINS OF A CAMPFIRE AND A TRAIL LEADING INLAND.

THIS LAND IS INHABITED.

WHO KNOWS WHAT WE WILL FIND? THESE PEOPLE COULD KILL US.

NOT KNOWING WHETHER THE NATIVES WOULD BE FRIENDLY OR **HOSTILE**, HE DID NOT WANT TO RISK THE LIVES OF HIS CREW. HE ORDERED HIS MEN BACK ABOARD THE SHIP. THIS WAS THE ONLY TIME CABOT SET FOOT ON LAND.

WE MUST NOT TAKE ANY CHANCES.

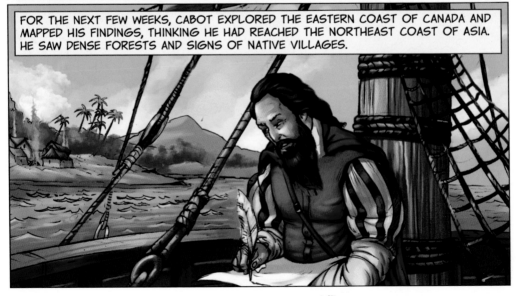

FOR THE NEXT FEW WEEKS, CABOT EXPLORED THE EASTERN COAST OF CANADA AND MAPPED HIS FINDINGS, THINKING HE HAD REACHED THE NORTHEAST COAST OF ASIA. HE SAW DENSE FORESTS AND SIGNS OF NATIVE VILLAGES.

THE SEA WAS SWARMING WITH FISH. THERE WERE SO MANY THAT THE MEN COULD CATCH THEM SIMPLY BY LOWERING BASKETS INTO THE WATER.

HIS MISSION COMPLETE, CABOT HEADED FOR HOME. THE *MATTHEW* ARRIVED BACK IN BRISTOL, ENGLAND, ON AUGUST 6, 1497. HIS SHIP WAS **INTACT**, AND CABOT HAD NOT LOST A SINGLE MEMBER OF HIS CREW.

CABOT IMMEDIATELY TOOK A COACH TO LONDON TO MEET WITH KING HENRY VII. THE COACH RIDE TOOK HIM THREE DAYS.

ENGLAND CANNOT PAY YOU ENOUGH.

IT IS MY HONOR TO SERVE YOU, YOUR HIGHNESS.

KING HENRY WAS EXCITED BY THE SUCCESS OF CABOT'S **EXPEDITION**. HE REWARDED CABOT WITH 10 POUNDS OF SILVER AND ANOTHER 20 POUNDS PER YEAR, WHICH WAS A VERY LARGE SUM IN THOSE DAYS.

THE WORLD IS NOW YOURS.

SPLENDID!

CABOT MADE A MAP AND A GLOBE OF HIS FINDINGS FOR THE KING. THE MAP AND GLOBE NO LONGER EXIST, NOR DO ANY RECORDS CABOT MADE OF HIS JOURNEY.

JOHN CABOT QUICKLY BECAME A NATIONAL HERO. HE WAS THE MAN WHO HAD DISCOVERED A NEW ROUTE TO ASIA FOR ENGLAND, OR SO THEY THOUGHT AT THE TIME.

ALL HAIL JOHN CABOT!

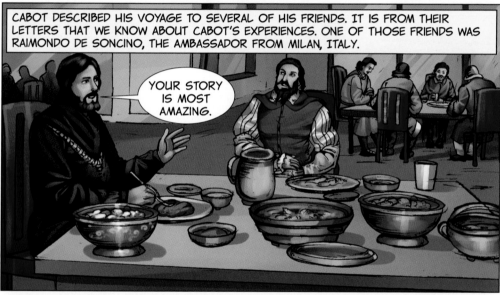

CABOT DESCRIBED HIS VOYAGE TO SEVERAL OF HIS FRIENDS. IT IS FROM THEIR LETTERS THAT WE KNOW ABOUT CABOT'S EXPERIENCES. ONE OF THOSE FRIENDS WAS RAIMONDO DE SONCINO, THE AMBASSADOR FROM MILAN, ITALY.

YOUR STORY IS MOST AMAZING.

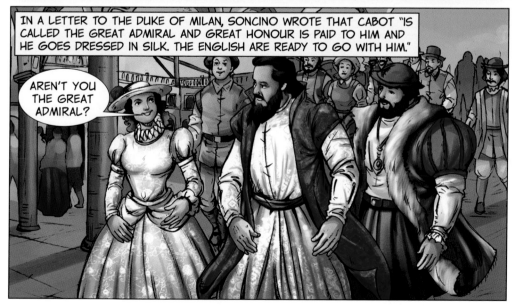

IN A LETTER TO THE DUKE OF MILAN, SONCINO WROTE THAT CABOT "IS CALLED THE GREAT ADMIRAL AND GREAT HONOUR IS PAID TO HIM AND HE GOES DRESSED IN SILK. THE ENGLISH ARE READY TO GO WITH HIM."

AREN'T YOU THE GREAT ADMIRAL?

KING HENRY WAS EAGER TO SEND CABOT TO SEA AGAIN ON A MUCH LARGER EXPEDITION.

YOU SHALL HAVE 10 ARMED SHIPS AND ALL THE CREW YOU NEED.

THE KING, HOWEVER, WAS SPENDING TOO MUCH MONEY PUTTING DOWN **REBELLIONS** IN ENGLAND. AFTER MONTHS OF PLANNING, HE DECIDED HE COULD NOT AFFORD A LARGE-SCALE EXPEDITION AND GAVE CABOT ONLY ONE SHIP.

SOME OF THE MERCHANTS OF BRISTOL RAISED ENOUGH MONEY FOR FOUR MORE SHIPS.

WE SHALL MAKE A FORTUNE OFF THE NEW TRADE ROUTES.

IN THE SPRING OF 1498, CABOT SET SAIL ON HIS THIRD AND FINAL VOYAGE. THIS TIME HE WOULD NOT BE SO LUCKY.

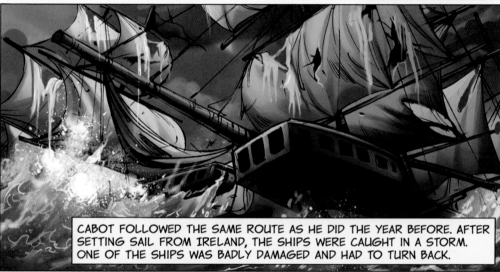

CABOT FOLLOWED THE SAME ROUTE AS HE DID THE YEAR BEFORE. AFTER SETTING SAIL FROM IRELAND, THE SHIPS WERE CAUGHT IN A STORM. ONE OF THE SHIPS WAS BADLY DAMAGED AND HAD TO TURN BACK.

THE REST OF THE SHIPS SAILED ON AND WERE NEVER HEARD FROM AGAIN. BY 1499, CABOT AND HIS CREW HAD BEEN GIVEN UP FOR DEAD.

HISTORIANS CAN ONLY GUESS WHAT HAPPENED TO CABOT AND HIS CREW.

HOLD STEADY, MEN!

THE SHIPS MIGHT HAVE BEEN WRECKED ON THE JAGGED ROCKS THAT LIE BENEATH THE WATER ALONG THE COAST OF CANADA.

WHAT NOW, CAPTAIN?

WE WILL LIVE OFF THE LAND.

CABOT AND HIS MEN MIGHT HAVE MADE IT TO CANADA, WHERE THEY EITHER STARVED OR WERE KILLED BY NATIVES. THERE IS EVIDENCE, HOWEVER, THAT CABOT REACHED CANADA.

IN 1500, TWO YEARS AFTER CABOT'S FINAL VOYAGE, A PORTUGUESE EXPLORER NAMED GASPAR CORTE REAL SAILED TO CANADA. HE FOUND PART OF A SWORD AND SOME SILVER RINGS THAT COULD ONLY HAVE COME FROM CABOT'S HOME COUNTRY OF ITALY.

MANY YEARS LATER, IN 1526, ANOTHER GREAT EXPLORER SET SAIL TO NORTH AMERICA FOR SPAIN. HIS ENGLISH NAME WAS SEBASTIAN CABOT, THE YOUNGEST SON OF JOHN CABOT.

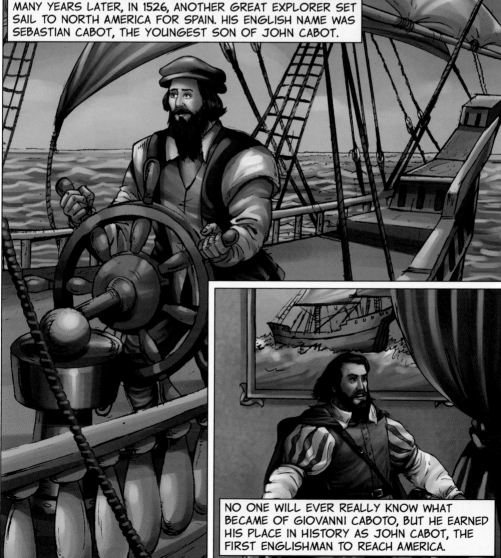

NO ONE WILL EVER REALLY KNOW WHAT BECAME OF GIOVANNI CABOTO, BUT HE EARNED HIS PLACE IN HISTORY AS JOHN CABOT, THE FIRST ENGLISHMAN TO REACH AMERICA.

Timeline and Map

c. 1450 John Cabot is born in Genoa, Italy, as Giovanni Caboto.

1474 Caboto marries Mattea. They have three sons named Ludovico, Sancto, and Sebastiano.

1492 Christopher Columbus sails the Atlantic Ocean and finds what he thinks is a new route to Asia.

1490s Caboto goes to see the kings of Spain and Portugal to ask them to finance a voyage, but his requests are denied.

c. 1490– 1495 Caboto moves his family to Bristol, England, where he becomes known as John Cabot.

1496 The English king, Henry VII, agrees to finance a voyage for Cabot. Cabot sets sail on his first voyage from Bristol. He does not get far and turns back.

1497 In May, Cabot sets sail on his second voyage from Bristol.

On June 24, Cabot arrives in what is now Newfoundland, Canada.

On August 6, Cabot arrives back in Bristol.

1498 In May, Cabot sets sail on his third voyage and is never seen again.

1500 Gaspar Corte Real, a Portuguese explorer, finds what might be the remains of Cabot's expedition.

1525 John Cabot's youngest son, Sebastian Cabot sails to the Americas in 1526.

Map of Cabot's Route

Glossary

ambassador (am-BA-suh-dur) The highest-ranking representative of one country assigned to conduct relations with another country.

apprentice (uh-PREN-tis) A person who learns a trade by working for someone who is already trained.

astrolabe (AS-truh-layb) An instrument that measures the positions of stars, used to find one's way on the oceans.

bearings (BER-ingz) Measurements taken that will tell the geographical position of a person or a thing.

expedition (ek-spuh-DIH-shun) A trip for a special purpose.

historians (hih-STOR-ee-unz) People who study the past.

hostile (HOS-tul) Unfriendly, relating to an enemy.

intact (in-TAKT) Not broken or damaged.

merchant (MER-chunt) Someone who owns a business that sells goods.

missions (MIH-shunz) Special jobs or tasks.

nautical (NAW-tih-kul) Relating to ships, navigation, and to sailing.

navigator (NA-vuh-gay-ter) A person who uses maps, the stars, or special tools to travel in a ship, an aircraft, or a rocket.

province (PRAH-vins) One of the main parts of a country.

quadrant (KWAH-drunt) An instrument for measuring the altitude of a star or of the Sun in order to find one's geographical position from the ocean.

rebellions (rih-BEL-yunz) Fights against one's government.

related (rih-LAYT-ed) Told something, such as a story.

Index

Websites

Due to the changing nature of Internet links, PowerKids Press has developed an online list of websites related to the subject of this book. This site is updated regularly. Please use this link to access the list:

www.powerkidslinks.com/jgff/cabo/